My Little prayers for all occasions

Published by iCharacter Ltd. (Ireland)
www.iCharacter.org
Copyright. All rights reserved.
By Agnes and Salem de Bezenac
Illustrated by Agnes de Bezenac
Colored by Fanny L.

Copyright © 2015 iCharacter Limited. All rights reserved. No part of this book may be reproduced in any form or by any electronic or mechanical means, including information storage and retrieval systems, without written permission from the publisher or author, except in the case of a reviewer, who may quote brief passages embodied in critical articles or in a review.

"Please and Thank You God",
Your works I do applaud!

When I'm still or on my way,
I can thank You every day.

prayers...

For those I love:
Mom, Dad, Grandma, Grandpa...

page **6**

When I need help:
When I am sick,
When I am alone,
When traveling...

page **14**

For Celebrations :
Birthdays, Christmas, Easter, New Year...

page **22**

During my day :
Wake up, breakfast, meals, at school, playtime...

page **36**

For Bedtime :
Sleep, peace, good dreams...

page **64**

Daddy & Mommy

Thank You

God, for my mommy and daddy that I love dearly. Thank You that they love me too, and take such good care of me and my whole family.

Please

give them strength, patience and wisdom when I sometimes give them a hard time. Please help me to "Honor and obey my parents in the Lord." Amen.

(Eph. 6:2)

Grandpa & Grandma

Thank You

God, for my grandma and grandpa that love me so much. Thank You for fun times we have together.
And I love it when they give me special treats.

Please

protect them and keep them healthy and strong. Please help them "Live a long life and many days in peace." Amen.

(Proverbs 3:1,2)

My friends

Thank you

dear Jesus, for being the best friend I could have. Thank You for all the times I also get to enjoy with my other friends that You have given me.

Please

help me to be thoughtful of my friends when they have a need. Please help me live the verse that says: "A friend loves at all times." Amen.

(Pro. 17:17)

My pets

Thank You

dear God, for making cute pets that bring me so much joy. Thank You that they're so much fun and keep me company when I'm alone.

Please

help them not to make too many messes in our house. Please keep Your promise that "None will fall to the ground." Amen.

(Mat. 10:29)

When I'm alone

Thank You

God, that even though I sometimes feel alone and don't know what to do, I can get ideas from You. Thank You that when there are no other distractions around, it gives me more time to spend with just You.

Please

help me to keep myself busy and happy by doing something useful. Please help me to remember that "You are always with me, right beside me." Amen.

(Psa. 16:8)

When I'm afraid

Thank You

God, that even when it's dark, I have my family around who loves me. Thank You that I don't have to be scared of monsters or bad dreams when You are near.

Please

help me to trust that everything will be okay and that I have nothing to fear. Please help me to learn that "When I am afraid, I can put my trust in You." Amen.

(Psa. 56:3)

When I'm Sick

Thank You

dear Jesus, that I am healthy most of the time and only sick occasionally. Thank You that while I am sick, I get lots of loving care from my family and loved ones.

Please

help me to get the rest that I need and good healthy food to help my body feel better soon. Please forgive all my sins and heal all my sickness", like Your Word says. Amen. (Psa. 103:3)

When I have problems

Thank You

God, that problems give me a chance to figure out solutions on how to do better next time. Thank You that others are willing to help me with my problems, when I can't figure them out on my own.

Please

help me to make wise choices and to learn from my mistakes. Please help me to learn that I can also "Turn my worries over to You, for You care for me." Amen.

(1Pet. 5:7)

Going on a trip

Thank You

God, that we have a good working vehicle to be able to go on this trip. Thank You that our driver is well rested, alert and concentrated.

please

keep us safe and free from accidents as we travel. Please keep Your promise that says "The Lord will keep your going out and coming home." Amen.

(Psa. 121:8)

My birthday

Thank You

God, that I'm bigger than I was last year. Look how I've grown! Thank You that You've made birthdays such a fun and special time, and I feel so loved.

Please

give me strength and courage as I start a new year, ready to experience and learn new things. Please help me to also "Grow in Your grace and get to know You better." Amen. (2Pet. 3:18)

christmas

Thank You

dear Jesus, that Christmas is a wonderful time to think about You and show You how much I love You. Thank You that it's a special time to spend with everyone in my family and also that it's a time for giving.

Please

help me not to get so busy with all the parties and activities that I forget to pray and spend time with You. Please help me to give You glory just like the angels sang "Glory to God in the Highest and Peace to men of good will!" Amen.

(Luke 2:14)

vacations

Thank You

God, for extra days of fun and play that I can enjoy during this vacation. Thank You that I have time to experience new things, go to different places, and play with friends.

Please

help me to be loving with my family and friends, as we spend more time together. Please help me to "Be full of joy because You have done great things for us." Amen.

(Psa. 126:3)

Easter

Thank You

dear Jesus, for suffering on the cross to save me from my sins. Thank You that You rose again and will stay alive in my heart forever.

Please

help me to share the good news of Easter with others. Please help me to "Rejoice in this hope of new life, through Your resurrection." Amen.

(1 Pet.1:3-4)

Thanksgiving

Thank You

God, for how You take care of me so faithfully, by providing what I need. Thank You that I can enjoy this special day with my family and that we can praise You for all that we're thankful for.

Please

help me to take some time to stop and to count all of those blessings that You send my way. Please help me to "Give thanks to You, for You are good and Your love lasts forever." Amen. (Psa. 107:1)

New Year's

Thank You

God, for the past year; and for all of the things that I have learned, experienced and enjoyed. Thank You for the happy times, the sad times and the times that drew me closer to You.

Please

help me to grow strong and healthy in body and to become a little more like You, in spirit. Please help me "To learn to do what pleases You and give me the strength to do it." Amen. (Phil. 2:13)

wake up time

Thank You

God, that You kept me safe through the night and that I feel well rested. Thank You for the many things that I can look forward to today.

Please

bless this day and help my actions to be pleasing to You. Please help me to learn a lot in this "day that You have made, and to rejoice and be glad in it." Amen.

(Psa. 118:24)

Breakfast time

Thank You

God, for this tasty food that will give me energy at the start of this day. Thank You that I can eat healthy foods that will help me grow strong and tall.

Please

make this food good for my body so that I can concentrate on my school work. Please help me as I "eat this bread and drink from this cup, to do it in remembrance of You." Amen.

(1 Cor. 11:24,25)

Dressing up

Thank You

God, for all the clothes that I can wear, that help keep me warm and comfortable. Thank You for all the different textures, patterns and colors that are made for different seasons and activities.

Please

help me to be faithful to keep them clean and tidy and to be a good steward of my clothes. Please help me to live Your Word that says "Put on the Lord Jesus Christ!" Amen. (Rom. 13:14)

prep for school

Thank You

God, for notebooks, pencils and rulers. Thank You, that I have hands that know how to pick things up, pack my bag and get ready.

Please

help me not to forget or lose anything that I need to bring to school today. Please help me to "Do all things with the strength that You give me." Amen.

(Phil. 4:13)

school time

Thank You

God, that it's another day to go to school and learn something new. Thank You, that when something is difficult for me, our teacher is there to help.

Please

Please help me to concentrate and focus on my work and projects. Please help me to be "... wise and listen so that I can grow in knowledge and guidance."

(Pro. 1:5)

Lunch time

Thank You

God, for all of the different kinds of foods and tastes that You've made for us to enjoy. Thank You, that You faithfully provide us with food to eat.

Please

help me to be cheerful and thankful, even if it's not my very favorite vegetable. Please help me to live Your Word that says "In everything give thanks to God." Amen.

(1 Thes. 5:18)

Tidying up

Thank You

God, that it feels so good to have a clean room and a tidy house. Thank You, that I can learn and practice cleaning up a little more each day.

Please

help me to be diligent in my responsibilities and to do them well. Please help me to live Your Word that says "Be faithful in the little things and I will bless you with more." Amen. (Luk. 16:10)

Brush teeth

Thank You

God, for my strong, white teeth. They remind me of how wonderfully You've made me. Thank You for my toothbrush that helps to scrub away all the bacteria and leftover foods.

Please

help me to build the good habit of brushing my teeth after every meal. Please help me to do a good job as I try to make them "white as snow". Amen.

(Psa. 51:7)

Indoor play

Thank You

God, for the fun times of play that I can enjoy. Thank You for being near me while I play. It's always more fun when You're there.

Please

help me to think about others and to show love. Then we can have a happy time, while sharing and giving. Please help us while we play, to "Love one another, because love comes from God." Amen.

(1 John 4:7a)

Homework time

Thank you

God, that homework helps me to review what I've learned at school so that I can remember it better. Thank You, that even though I don't enjoy it so much, I can get it done quickly.

Please

help me to focus on what I'm doing and not get distracted with wanting to play. Please help me to "… do my best to be a good worker at my studies." Amen.

(2 Tim. 2:15)

snack time

Thank You

God, for quick snack foods that I enjoy. They keep me going till the next meal. Thank You, that I can also take pleasure in tasty, sweet treats once in awhile.

Please

help me to take advantage of healthy snacks that You've made, like juicy fruits or crunchy nuts. Please help me "Whenever I eat or drink or whatever I do, to do it all to Your glory." Amen. (1 Cor. 10:31)

outdoor play

Thank you

God for Your beautiful creation that I can enjoy. I breathe the fresh air, I smell the roses, I hear the birds sing. All that reminds me of Your greatness. Thank You for keeping me safe and free from harm.

please

help me to be alert and attentive, so that I don't do something dangerous. Please help "Your angels to guard and protect me." Amen. (Psa. 91:11)

Bath time

Thank You

God, for water, shampoo, bubbles and nice smelling soaps. Thank You, for my warm towel that dries me up so that I don't get cold afterwards.

Please

help me not to fall and hurt myself on the slippery floor. Please, keep me clean on the inside too, like your Word says "Now we are clean through the Word." Amen.

(John 15:3)

Dinner time

Thank you

God, for this meal to end the day. I feel so blessed that I have everything I need. Thank You that my tummy enjoys is so much and that it will last me all night long.

Please

help those who have less than I have to still have enough to eat tonight. Please, as I "... show my thankfulness, bless my food and water." Amen.

(Exo. 23:25)

Bed time

Thank You

God, for my warm, cozy, soft bed and for the pillow under my head. Thank You for everything I did and learned today and for the fun times of play.

Please

bless my night with pleasant and loving dreams. Please keep Your promise that says, "He gives his beloved rest." Amen.

(Psa. 127:2)

The sun sets

Thank You

God, that I enjoyed the day with lots of fun and play.

Thank You that You told the sun never to stay away.

Please

help me to settle down after all of the excitement and fun.

Please help me to realize that the day is now done.

prep for bed

Thank You

God, for water to brush my teeth and take a bath.

Thank You, for my towel that tickles my toes and makes me laugh.

Please

help me as I wash, get fresh and smell clean.

Please help my teddy to see that I have good hygiene.

Story Time

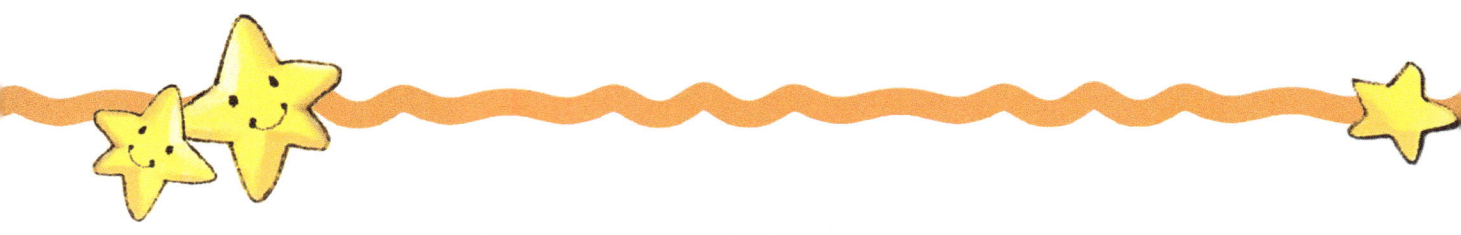

Thank You

God, for oodles of stories and books on my shelf.

Thank You for Mom and Dad so that I don't have to read by myself.

Please

help me to remember the stories that have lesson-filled parts.

Please keep us thinking of You as we hide these Words in our hearts.

Love and Cuddles

Thank You

God, for a sweet mom and dad who love me so.

Thank You that they give me cuddles to let me know.

Please

help me to show them lots of love in return.

Please help me to give the biggest hugs now that it's my turn.

Loved ones

Thank You

God, for grandparents, brothers and sisters.

Thank You, for my puppy, canary and kitten that purrs.

Please

keep them in Your loving care wherever they may be.

Please keep each one close to You now, and for eternity.

protection

Thank You

God, for keeping me safe while I lay here.

Thank You for being with me and that I have nothing to fear.

Please

protect me from dangers, worries and frights.

Please help me feel at peace, even as we switch off the lights.

pleasant dreams

Thank You

God, for giving me dreams that are pleasant.

Thank You that while I sleep, You are present.

Please

keep my thoughts and dreams, good and true.

Please keep away anything that would make me feel blue.

A cozy bed

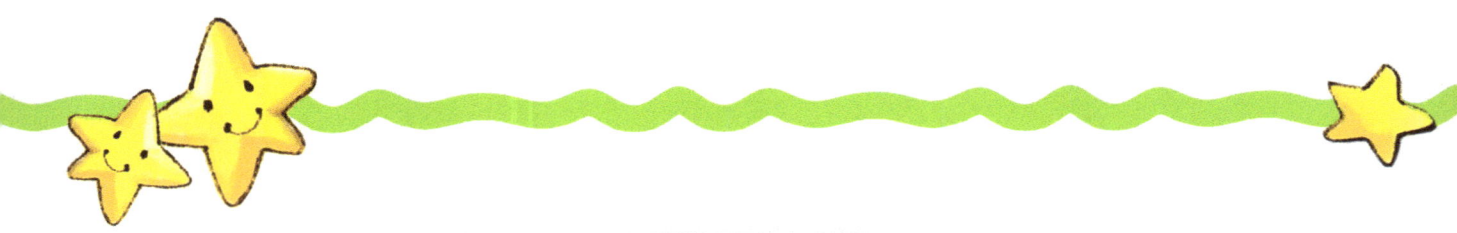

Thank You

God, that I have a warm, cozy, soft bed.

Thank You for a fluffy pillow where I can rest my head.

Please

give all the children in the world, a bed as comfy as mine.

Please help me to remember how blessed I am; I need not ever whine.

Night Noises

Thank You

God, that I can rest while everything is quiet and still.

Thank You, that even with odd little noises, my heart with peace You fill.

Please

help me not to worry about the sounds I hear.

Instead, I'll listen to You whisper in my ear.

Angels

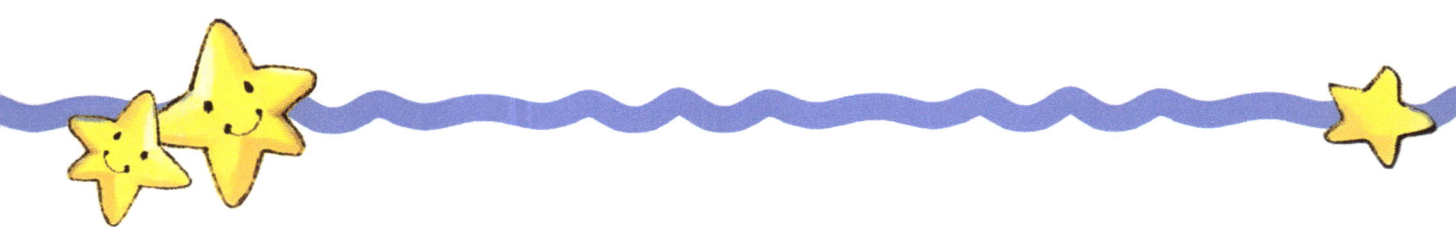

Thank You

God for Your angels
that guard and care.

Thank You, that they never leave
my side; they're always there.

Please

keep them strong, full
of courage and might.

Please help the things that I do
to bring them joy and delight.

Animals at Night

Thank You

God, for making animals that hunt at night.

Thank You that You made them with amazing eyesight.

Please

help them to find enough food for their babies.

Whether flying insects, crawling creatures or juicy berries.

Night Workers

Thank You

God, for the people who work while we sleep.

Thank You for the ones who guard, catch fish or watch sheep.

Please

bless them for being willing to work at night.

Please keep them wide awake as they check that everything's alright.

I can't sleep

Thank You

God that I've had an active day of play.

Thank You that You made the night as a way to end my day.

Please

help me to get calm even when I still feel full of energy.

Please help me to settle down, so I can think about You and rest my body.

Night Fears

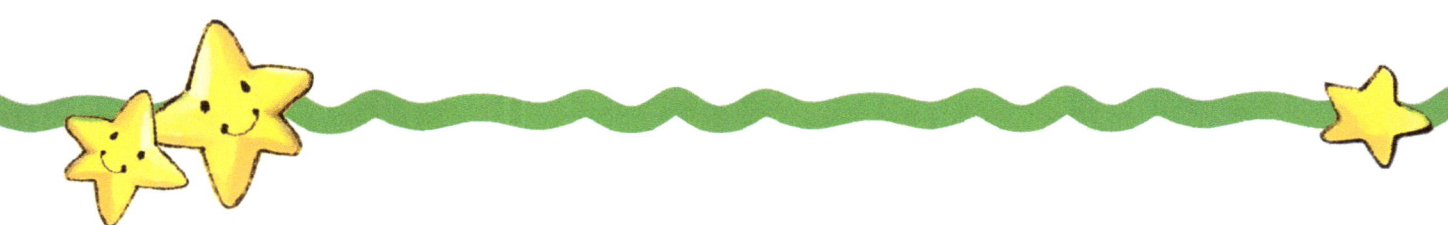

Thank You

God, that I don't have to be afraid of rushes in the breeze.

Thank You that shadows don't have to be scary, everyone agrees.

Please

help me to remember that I am safe in Your arms.

Please give me peaceful thoughts with no fears or alarms.

Moon and Stars

Thank you

God, for making the moon to light up the sky at night.

Thank You for the shining stars that are so tranquil and yet, an amazing sight.

Please

make me to be like one of Your stars, shining in the World that's dark.

Please make me kind and loving, and show me the best way to start.

A time to cuddle,
A time to love;
A time to pray
To your Father above.